Everyone Loves The Situation

Snooki: *I'm not white.*
JWoww: *What are you?*
Snooki: *Tan.*

Everyone Loves The Situation

Michael Cirelli

pen
man
ship

Penmanship Books
Brooklyn, NY

Penmanship Books

Published by Penmanship Publishing Group

593 Vanderbilt Avenue, #265
Brooklyn, NY 11238

www.penmanshipbooks.com

Printed in The United States of America

10 9 8 7 6 5 4 3 2 1

Cover & Author Photo: Syreeta McFadden

Cover Design: Jason Lalor

Grateful acknowledgement is made to the editors of the following publications where these poems first appeared: *Hanging Loose #98*: "5 Grenades (Homage & Apology)," "The Shirt Before the Shirt," "Variations on a Pazmanian Ghazal," and "The Blowout," *Muzzle Magazine*: "Half a Heroic Crown for Vin." "The Situation" was made into an animated short by Greta Scheing and premiered at the Pawtucket Arts Festival. "Little Waves" is a collaboration between the author, and poet F. Douglas Brown. Brown is a Cave Canem and a Kundiman fellow who teaches English at Loyola High School of Los Angeles, an all boys Jesuit school. "Little Waves" are written by the author, with all layout and creative design by Brown.

The author would also like to thank Mahogany L. Browne, Tonya Ingram, Syreeta McFadden, Peter Covino, Mac Barrett, F. Douglas Brown, Maria Lisella, Jon Sands, Cousin Vin, Cousin Cerissa, Cousin Layne, Cousin Jackie, Cousin Brit, Cousin Mel, Amanda and Kenny Cap, my Hambone, my Nana, my Bomb, and my Mom, my Dad, the Mangiones and the Cirellis (RIP).

First Penmanship trade edition: March 2011

ISBN# 978-0-9831219-3-0

for my cousin,
Vincent Joseph Cirelli III

Contents

Fan Club

The wallpaper
in my sister's bedroom
is turning Jonas.
The soil under my aunt's
feet is not Providence,
but Red Sox Nation.
There's the Whitman Star.
There's a sword with a blade
made of pure light.
We dress like Skywalkers
to uproot death's poem,
and spray our skin
white to walk on the moon.
For my anorak rendition:
I open my raised fist
to hold a remote control,
to point it at MTV's *Jersey Shore*,
to forget all about mission
statements, or what
they say. I'm JFK with bling on.
In my fanboy sequester:
I write poems for my cousins.
The kids on the TV
are cartoons of my family,
but without the city job
my grandfather died for,
or the rock
of heroin that keeps
rolling down The Hill.
When I ask cousin

Vinny if he knows the character
from our small state,
Pauly D,
he responds, "yeah I know him,
he's a goof, but he's in my fan club"—
Heart of Darkness
has a fan club, and all
the members dress as rivers.
I know what a groupie
of the WD-40 Fan Club looks
like because America
has taught me well
how to stereotype.
At Vin's Convention,
the fans are costumed
as strippers, bartenders,
twin nuns. The disco ball
in The Grand Ballroom
is not a disco ball
but a Death Star.
We smash it like a piñata
until our parents
spill out onto the dance floor.

I was born and raised a guido. It's just a lifestyle. It's being Italian. It's representin' family, friends, tanning, gel, everything. I got a fucking tanning bed in my place, that's how serious I am about being a guido and living up to that lifestyle. It takes me about 25 minutes to do my hair. It comes out perfect every single time.[1]

Pauly D Lives Up to The Lifestyle

There's a gateway, an arch
Over Atwells Avenue,
The entrance to Italian America,
And from it hangs "La Pigna,"
The pine comb,
A traditional symbol of abundance
For our people,
Who came to Federal Hill
And marched down this street
Each Columbus Day,
Who made bread and played bocce
In the Nocabulabet Bocce League,
Who hauled coal and branzino and
Valeted cars and delivered "apizza"
(In rain, sleet and slurs),
Up and down this avenue
That if followed far enough
Leads to the columned homes
Of Johnston—and lodged within
Those gaudy columns
Is the understanding that we made it,
As if getting from Providence to Johnston
Was like Sinatra conquering
New York, and all along Atwells Ave
The New World's billboards
Told us what we wanted
What we needed

---

1 "A New Family." Paul "Pauly D" DelVecchio. *Jersey Shore*. MTV. Season 1, Episode 1. 3 Dec. 2009.

(To fit in), as we polished our Cadillacs
and we wrapped Egyptian gold
Around our necks,
As we mistranslated the hard tongue
Of L'America and became
Our own new breed, abundantly
Gelled abundantly tanned,
Perfecting the lifestyle
In front of a beveled mirror,
Mistaking a pine comb
For a pineapple.

The Situation

He lifts his shirt
Exposing a tortoise shell,
Calls it: "The Situation."
Redefine it: abs,
Color it: melanin spray paint,
Grammar it: 3rd person
Nickname fitted with
A definite article capitalized:
Mike "The Situation,"
Not Mike "The Plumber"
Or Mike "The Stromboli"
(Which would better
Suit me). Mike claims
Everyone loves
The Situation: babies, dogs,
Hot girls, cougars, end quote.
When I hear the term
Now, I see each syllable of
Hair crisp as Sicilian crust,
Threaded eyebrows,
Pumpkin skin tone, can't wipe
Mike off that word—
"The situation at hand"
Translates into a palmful of ass.
"Situation Normal All
Fouled Up" becomes six cans
Of Coors Light.
"The Situation Room" is round,
And filled with hot water.
"The situation in the Middle East"

Has you there, grilling
Steaks and steaming lobsters
In a cyclone of dust.
When I need to understand
The situation, Mike exits
The self-esteem room,
Sews line after sweaty line
Into the ears of any Guidette
With ears, a situation
(Tragi)comedy that needs no translation.

If

one thing leads to another,
she said, I'm not gonna tell him
to get off. Gonna let him
climb my body like a lifeguard
chair and rub the orange
off my ass till I'm whiter than Virginia
Slims. Gonna make a plus sign
and *thank god!* for how far we've come:
sidestepped bunk crops
and Tyranny in the Old Country
to hop ship to Ellis Island
where we came in Black, black
as squid ink and cranked
the race spigot till semolina mirrored
our skin—and my great grandfather
had coal under the tongue
and my Nonna used rationed
Romas cut with water to stretch
the sauce and my grandfather
built an oven that my father stoked
with anthracite and he met my mother,
The Belle of Poughkeepsie,
and because he climbed atop her
one night when the sky was on smoke
break, they could have me, their daughter.

Pauly D Brings the Flowerbed

When he couldn't fit
The tanning bed
Out of his basement door
To take with him
To the summer beach house,
Pauly went into his mother's
Garden and dug out
A 4 x 6 (and 3 inches thick)
Blanket of flowers
To lay over him at night
(Instead of fluorescent
Lights) to remind him
Of home, so that he could
Close his eyes and feel
The roots tickle his paling skin.

Variations on a Rhyming Italian Mom Ghazal

She roasts the sausage, bakes the ziti, pounds the cutlets (pounds them
Hard), don't forget the broccoli rabe, she's a certified Italian mom.

Peel the garlic, turn the sod, basil blooming in the yard, tomatoes, zukes,
Cukes and squash—fresh from the garden of an Italian mom.

Stale bread becomes croutons, then oreganata to top the cod,
Whatever's left turns minestrone, the alchemy of an Italian mommy.

Between each course the boys take naps, she clears the plates and
Prepares the next: lobster, clams, homemade pasta, and the Old
        Canteen's steak a la Mama.

As sauces simmer, she sweeps the kitchen, wipes the counter, while
Auntie's bitchin', she sprays the bathroom, scrubs the john, the work's never
        done for an Italian mom.

She cooks, she cleans, she does the laundry, babysits for Cousin Bobby,
Serving men's a full time job, no rest for the weary Italian mom.

They can't work an iron or lift a plate, or make the bed they sleep in late,
She's raised a bunch of friggin' slobs, the cross she bears as their Italian mom.

All she asked was to grab dessert, a pie, a cake, on the way home from
Work, what he got was rather woeful: a cardboard box of chocolate Yodels?

Spent all her life making supper— love's the work of an Italian mother—
What made her toil that much harder, was putting up with an Italian father.

Snooki™

Not Turtle Island, nor Sedona's
Vortex, but Seaside Heights,
But Atlantic City and 3 sevens,
From Staten Island to the Northern
Kingdom, from a line of Remuses,
And a branch of suckling wolves,
Her people who are not her
People, but she suckled anyway,
She took names regardless, wedged
A half moon beneath The Pouf
(A headdress) of black silk, black
As the pupil of Horus—two arcs
Above the brows, two ancient
Hieroglyphs meaning: hills for olives
Hills for lemons hills for sacrifice,
But no temple, no monastery
But shore house, no Dharmasala
And prayer beads, nor Easter Island
But a golden cross, still sacred work
Here, still 16 symbols, as she paints her face,
As she clips, clamps and fastens
Each adornment before heading to
The United States Patent and Trademark
Office on February 7th, before forking over
A stack of pyramids and making
That name hers.

The Blowout

The blowout is ancient mathematics.
Is hyperbolic, is secrets of standing
Obelisks after time's constant fist pump.
Blowout is re-animate wind, kicked out
Of the Mediterranean. Blowout lands
In Johnston Rhode Island where the last
Note of the last names is: –echhio
Or –elli or –freddi/o. More Italian-Americans
Here than anywhere on the planet.
Blowout masters the shape of flame,
Masters the direction of against-move-
Ment, masters fright reflex. The blowout
Teaches the follicles homo erectus,
Teaches the follicles *attention!,* teaches
Perpendicular. The hair has multiple proofs:
Wind, water, soccer, motorcycle, Pauly postulates.
Like frogs the boys party hop from
Boat to boat and Pauly's blowout, in-and-out
Of the water all day, he said, didn't move an inch.
The ozone is opening her mouth like
A blue fish as 1,000 blowdryers are culling
Shapes on the heads of Johnston's sons,
Shapes like the crests of waves in the Ocean
State, shapes like a dollop of Cool
Whip on an anchor.

Dancing with the Stars

after Michael Cirelli

I've never slow danced
with a white dwarf, or Humptied
in a blast of luminosity.
Closest I got, with the blondest Gretchen,
7th grade Sadie Hawkins Dance,
"Stairway to Heaven,"
and my hips hinged like >,
hiding the growing telescope
in my Gap jeans. To talk stars
is to talk spectra, to classify
something by what it absorbs.
Star so sponge-like.
Star so human-like, star with
wishing well-nature I suppose.
To talk stars is to talk travel.
Star so 3 Wise Men-like, who also
followed a star.
On the show, stars disguised as
broken football players, stars
with comedian makeup on,
and stars of reality
Audrina Patridge, Bristol Palin,
Mike "The Situation," Cha Cha
Cha, Viennese Waltz and Rumba
off beat to the beat. If only Mike could
show off his Fist Pump, if only The Hoff
could do the Slow-Mo-Beach-Trot
in a crotch sling. That might be more

worthy of Xi Draconis, Gamma Tauri,
Jabhat al Acrab. Or maybe not.
Star so flaw-like. So traveled
and weary. Star only a star
because of our eyes. More eyes,
more star-like. Star so easy like the top of:

1 E J K L P
2 Z S T Q R
3 V T B A C Q
4 S M Z A E T L Y
5 D W G U I O P N
6 H F Y T G J K M L P
7 Z X C E T Y W J K A S M B I

It's because you're Line 1
in the public gaze, star.
It's because we can look up and
see you, spoon, can read you in the night sky.
Can read you all over the TV
and the blogs, star.
It's because I dance here reader,
this language two-step,
because you see me see my Line 1and my Line 54,
dear friend, that I've transformed
into this star, this smudged *,
this slipshod faulty satellite I've dressed
up as a star.

Life Change

In a cosmos
Where a fried pickle
Can be a life
Changing experience[2]—
When I was
Her age
I wanted to change
My life. I moved
To Brum, in the bull's eye
Of a mental hospital,
And from the light fixture
In a small bedroom
Above me
Hung a man
Who did not glow.
Life changing.
I camped in Plum Village.
I fixed hearts in Poland.
I flashed America
For first class access
And monks remember
My name. Life changing.
I glued prayer wheels. Buried
Tomato seeds, like time
Capsules. Inked my skin
To not forget,

---

[2] *This puts pickles on a whole 'nother level. It's like a sliced pickle, but it was fried. It was crunchy, but it was juicy. Eating fried pickles was a life-changing experience.* "Going South." Nicole "Snooki" Polizzi. *Jersey Shore*. MTV. Season 2, Episode 1. 29 July 2010.

A pictograph
Shooting fire from its nostrils—
Sixteen years later,
On the backside
Of a two-way mirror
There's a couch.
There's a TV trying for amnesia.
There's four empty cans
Of Pringles, a body
Echoing the moon:
Starved and gorged.
It's browning under MTV's
Infrared heat lamp.
Sixteen years late,
I fly back to Brum and visit graves.
I drive a thumbtack
Through a place on a map
Where monks can feel
My thumbprint
In the glue.

100 Names for Nicole

the history of a name, for Nicole "Snooki" Polizzi

Your mother wrote them in the sand
Before you were born
Spanish for *sea*
Spanish for *light*
Spanish for *star*
Before she had to give you up
And you became
Little bird in Spanish
Or *steel bird* in Spanish
Or *better life*
En Ingles
Your mother's last gift
When she presented you to Los Estados Unidos
Presented you to Arboles de Dinero
Presented you to Leche y Miel y McDonald's where
You became *Pequeña Minnie Mouse*
Became *Nieve Blanca*
Became more names for loss than Inuit snow
Then nada
And when America opened her arms
For Native America to call you
Cree for *Daughter of Moon*
Algonquin for *Tracking the Starlight*
(And later) *Dances with Gorillas* in Seminole
Or *Cartwheels Under Disco Ball* in Narragansett
The Polizzis had mortgaged a foundation of bones
To sit upon like birthday candles and knit
You a tiny pink sweater and

Name you *Nicole*
(A name not on your mother's list)
Nicole Polizzi
And you wore that name
As your uncles called you *sweetheart* in Italian
Called you *darling* in Italian
And you mixed leopard and mixed rhinestones and
Mixed a tiara of black sprayed hair with that Italian
And claimed the title *Guidette*
Claimed the title *Tan*
Took the nickname *Snooki* and *Snickers* and *Schnooks*
And *Snooks* and *Schnickens*
When you went to school and went to malls
And went to clubs
And stuck your tongue deep into boys' faces and stuck
Your finger deep down your throat
To be named *consumer* in American
To be named *slut* in Patriarchy
To be named *bulimic* in American
All listed in the *First World Baby Names* book
Where stacked beneath you
Are a hundred names
Are a hundred sparkling badges
Names that mean *lobster advocate*
Names that mean *pickle connoisseur*
That mean *she is not a hamster she is not a trashbag*
Pilgrimess of the 20s
Lover of the good-guy-jerk-off
Princess of the pouf
Names for *manicures* and *bronzers* and *melanin* and names
For *daughter*—
As your mother in Chile whispers
The names on her list

Spanish for *angel*
Spanish for *consolation*
Spanish for *sorrows*
Spanish for *God is my judge*
Until her lips turn blue.

GTL

The formula for success
in Darfur: hide from
the Janjaweed,
tie the girls to balloons
and let go. Success in Palestine
equals Israel antonyming
South Africa (1912-1994).
Equals analogies to sharing.
Juarez needs the antidote
for disappearing ~~ink~~
women and
Pakistan needs "Big Yellow Taxi"
played backwards
before it turns Baghdad.
In order to be successful
in a Drake song
you want the money, money
and the cars, cars and the clothes,
the hos I suppose.
In Dubai: cranes, Louis hijab.
Afghanistan: a Flux Capacitor.
In Japan: teenage underwear
dispensers, Ahi. Ethiopia-Djibouti-
Cambodia-Somalia-et-al: ~~rice~~
Rice. At The Jersey Shore,
it's G-T-L: Gym, Tan, Laundry—
Maintain the cuts all over
the torso. Darken the complex-
ion under the chemistry
of light bulbs. The t-shirts, with spades

all over them, need to be
bedazzled in sequined
knockoff blood diamonds.
That way you can look mint
and creep on all
the skeletons at Karma.

Like Hello

Yes I had sex,
She said,
Like hello, you're gonna
Have sex if you're
Into someone.
Sixty years ago,
When the cars looked
Like spacecraft,
Seaside Heights
Lined up lacquered planks
Of wood for couples to walk
Down and gaze into the Atlantic,
— dotted with steamships —
Hand, a saucer, in hand, a teacup,
And the ladies
Had frilly umbrellas
And the men were called
Mister and the Mrs. *Ma'am*
And maybe at the end
Was a kiss (on the cheek)
Before he drops her off
To Mr. and Mrs. Castiglio
And thanks them for allowing
Him to take Samantha
To the boardwalk for sherbets.
Nowadays it's just
Wham bam — not even
A thank you — ma'am.

Half & Half

Half the night she hooked
Up with "The Situation" and half
With Ronnie. Mike was burnt
Onions trying to play it off
Spring. Sammi "Sweetheart"
Made her choice, sautéed
Till translucent. Maybe half
Her life she loved cats and half
She loved catnip. Or half
The time at school she paid
Attention and half she applied
Eyeliner. Half of her body
May be bitter, but all of her heart
Is sweet. Tonight Sammi chose
Ronnie, Ronnie Oh Ronnie,
And rolled her tongue deep
Down his throat like a drain stick.
Sure, thirty minutes earlier
She was making out with Mike,
But that was the first half of the night,
The half of the night that's just milk
To an evening filled with heavy cream.

I wanna marry a guido. My ultimate dream is to move to Jersey, find a nice juiced hot tanned guy, and live my life.[3]

Famous Pajamas

There were boom mics &
reporters hovering over
the most famous pajamas,
John & Yoko
each holding a flower
singing "Give Peace a Chance"
in the presidential suite
in white cotton.
Ironically, band mate Paul
composed "Yesterday"
in bed (not Bed-in),
and woke up hung over
with a shadow hanging over him
and no pajamas, just skin.
When MLK had a dream,
his pajamas should have been
Kevlar,
instead of clay pigeon.
Notorious B.I.G.
never dreamed
hip-hop would take it this far
as he slept on his mother's couch
in a flannel onesie,
the pestle
in his stomach grinding
down
sardines,
the zillion stars

[3] "A New Family." Nicole "Snooki" Polizzi. *Jersey Shore*. MTV. Season 1, Episode1. 3 Dec. 2009.

over St. James & Fulton
waving their hands like
deaf applause.
Friedrich August Kekulé
von Stradonitz
dreamt a perfect benzene structure
in starched white polyester
and Barack Hussein Obama
inherited dreams from his father
in b-ball shorts doubling as
pjs. Snooki's famous pajamas
are silk leopards,
her slippers pink bunnies,
and the comforter she pulls
over her pouf is soft as
New Jersey stack smoke
when she closes her eyes
after another long shift
at the party
and dreams
of the ultimate guido.

Looney Tunes

You are a stumpy bastard.
You with your Fred Flintstone toe,
Your doorstop big toe. Your
Toe made of wood,
Carved into a scalene triangle
Instead of a mallard. Your
Stump fledgling branches
For arms like a snowman,
Your stump with too many rings
For your age. Stump
Smuggling a cockeyed pyramid.
I want to tell Porky
Pig that trap doors are real.
I fell in one one night and woke up
With exaggerated white-gloved hands
On the set of Halloween.
Woke up in the hull of a Grand
Canyon, having a nose they wanted
To grow that did not grow.
In Times Square, a man who speaks
Mandarin draws a caricature
Of me and my flat-chested lady.
In the drawing, she wears huge boobs,
Her purse has a charcoal dollar
Sign on it, and her boyfriend
Is a coyote.

Half a Heroic Crown for Vin

I.

My cousin Vinny looks up
to me like I'm a gold-plated
statue on the top of a State
House made of books.
Like a comet dragging a fiery
tassel. Like a seagull filled
with ink. He doesn't know, I look
up to him too: his hard smirk
that's taken a punch. His realness
I long for. I'm a wannabe Vinny—
When I'm brave enough for a fight,
I wear a helmet, and ice skates.
When I feel like talking shit, I stay
inside the car, with the windows up.

II.

With the windows up, we drove
in silence to The Hill to get my dying
father jumbo shrimp cocktail.
Vin was always on call for Uncle Guido.
On our way back to the car, two guidos
ran up on us. Vin went down
the alley with one, while the other held
my arm, Jesus on his ripped right tricep.
Wait, he said. I did, we watched, they circled:
the Tale of the Tape being worked out like
fast math in their heads. I wanted to charge

the alley, but I didn't want to charge
the alley, and I didn't. Vin drew a knife
and before I knew it, we were back in the car.

III.

We were back in the car heading
to the hospital with a half-dozen shrimp.
Vin was cool as cocktail sauce, cooler
than don't-give-a-fuck. Vin was all
live by the streets, die by the streets
as his mother followed above
in the shape of a crow. Little cousin:
growing into my father's fading shadow,
eating the poison from his failing organs.
Rubbernecking every girl we passed,
Vin sped down Atwells Ave in a Honda Accord
that reeked of the ocean. Just like dad would,
he parked right in front of the Emergency Room
not giving a fuck.

IV.

Not giving a fuck is a symptom
of tough, depending on who holds it
between their stained fingers.
It burns cigarette holes into a cheek.
It doesn't care who you are or what
you do or who you know. My hero
once punched a guy, who was on
the other side of a window. Left hyphens
all over his face from the glass. But that was in '74,
when only cops had guns. Kids these days

are scared as hell, and gunning for a Vin
to earn a stripe. One night, when the club
floor musta been slanted, a champagne glass
perforated Vincent's neck.

V.

Vincent's neck had a gauze patch
blotted with a red Rorschach
that traced a silhouette of Uncle Guido,
and he told me it was: "*nothin,*" *some goof*
threw a glass in tha club. I remember
"nothin" as a kid: waiting in the backseat
of a Lincoln Town Car in a project parking lot.
Stopping to get Pixie Sticks and watching
my father pour the blue sugar onto the street.
Vin was Uncle Guido's apprentice.
When I hear him say "*nothin,*" I remember
my father pulling a fork from his stomach
at the beach house. On his deathbed,
I remember him crying out for his mother.

VI.

Crying for his mother, Vin still looked
tough as hell. I'd never seen him cry
until that day in front of her polished casket.
Vin's mom was my mom's best friend.
They grew up together dodging Italian boys.
Used to smoke Salem's on the highway overpass
and spit on the cars below singing "*I will survive*"
because of our fathers. My mom married
in first and his mom soon followed, except

his mom left a different way, slid out one night
in a dream. Vin carved her into his arm.
Vin preserved his mother's son under a mural
of religious tattoos. Grandma complained, *ya got Jesus*
all over ya, and you don't even go to church.

VII.

You don't even go to church
but you pray, a request engraved
around your neck: **God forgive me**.
When I tell him I ask that too, he looks
surprised, because he looks up to me.
Like perpendicular pencils on the top
of a cathedral. Like a flag made of paper.
I can do no wrong. When he drapes an archangel
across his back, of course it's Michael,
with a sword puncturing the devil.
I tell Vinny that the spider web on his elbow
is not a spider web, but a dream catcher.
That the anchor tattooed on mine is not
an anchor, but an arrow chasing Hope.

Fighting

Since the time when
Fishes started to bleed
Their image into rock,
When fire was the hottest
Thing on the market,
We've been fighting.
We called god by 42 names
So we could fight.
We called your grass greener
So we could incinerate you.
We froze ice and made skates
To punch your lights out.
When people have no water
They fight, no food they fight.
When a tank crushes
Your ancient olive trees
There is no other option than
To fight. Two people say
God exactly the same, but disagree
On a lineage, so they blow
Each other up. At the Jersey Shore
The boys are well fed,
And the olive oil is abundant.
They all say *God* exactly the same.
Say *what a view*. Say *yum*.
I don't understand why they
Fight so much. Don't understand
How a fist can land on a girl's
Jaw like an explorer, like a hippo-
Pota-kiss, or how

Ronnie can brawl after a moonlit
Stroll down the boardwalk. I wanna
Scribble myself in pixel and climb
Into the box. Slide a fork
Into one fist, a tablespoon into
The other fist and dangle a plate
Of linguine with clam sauce
In front of their bruised faces.

I see a bunch of gorilla juiceheads. Tall, completely jacked, steroids, like multiple growth hormones. That's, like, the type that I'm attracted to.[4]

Gorilla Juicehead Rhymed Couplets

He's a lamb inside a gorilla suit.
His shepherd is a dumbbell.

He drinks a Super-Sized gorilla juice.
Flash a needle and his bum swells.

He's a doe behind a lion mask.
An aardvark snorting Creatine.

Ground horse hooves in his powderflask.
Flip-flops, wifebeater, and a Jesus piece.

His stomach copy cats an alligator's.
His arms are wide as Roman columns.

He revs a Lincoln Navigator.
Beneath his roar's a squealing possum.

Grizzly pulp, the rind of sharks—
Ripe hormones for his smoothies.

He makes his cat calls with a bark.
GTL's his daily routine.

A tanning bed burns brain cells.
Gel formalde-hides a piglet.

---

4 "That's How the Shore Goes." Jenni "JWoww" Farley. *Jersey Shore.* MTV. Season 1-Finale, Episode 9. 21 Jan. 2010.

His body's hard as walnut shells,
But the nut is soft as giblets.

He's a koala in a rhino tux.
He's an ostrich with a hammerhead.

In every single sport he sucks.
He compensates by lifting lead.

Before the meat went to his skull,
He was a scrawny little newt.

After the twinkle in a bull,
He was a zygote in a mom suit.

Muscle Milk in the Rider

Prince requests a physician to give him an injection of Vitamin B-12 before he reigns stage. In Van Halen's rider, they demand a bowl of M&M's with all the brown ones removed, like a metaphor for grad school. Mariah "doesn't do stairs," much like greyhounds at the racetrack. She also requests rabbits, puppies and kittens to keep her company. Derrick's not a rock star but a poet, and in his first ever rider he asked for a yo-yo, which means: Toy Imitates Life in my language. Iggy Pop's rider has an addendum called "Dead Dog Island," which means: Landmass Imitates Life in my language. Instead of tea, ginger, lemon, instead of pails full of vodka, when Ronnie makes his club appearances, he needs "six bottles of Muscle Milk" in his rider. The protein screams in his neck vein as he pounds the air above the mezz with his fist. If I had a rider, I'd request a first edition Qur'an. Dad's eggplant parm. A beach chair. I'd ask for an Argentinean jockey, someone who could *ya ya ya* all around the green room, someone who could hop on my back and race me to the finish.

An Oft Overlooked Point Regarding The Don

for All Aspiring Mobsters

Michael Corleone went to Dartmouth.

Variations on a Pazmanian Ghazal

Vinny "The Pazmanian Devil" Pazienza was our Rocky.
Every kid wanted to be like Stallone, but we all wanted to simile Paz.

The Paz wasn't from Pazmania, but from Cranston RI,
Where he sat in his gym studying films of Rocky.

Vinny Paz was half-showboat-half-freight train,
Half-Sinatra-half-Balboa: all Italian Stallion.

Vinny mastered roundhouse, mastered Playboy Mansion,
Was Prince of Providence Civic Center, where they pumped
the theme song from Rocky.

After the car accident, the doctor told Vinny he would never
Fight again. Instead, Paz acted like Rocky in Rocky V.

RI's favorite son, The Pazmanian Devil returned to the gym
Bolted to a back brace and halo: RI's Roman Catholic angel.

When he climbed back into the ring it was like a movie or
A dream, in less than a year, Paz went from bedpans to Rambo.

Vinny piloted tassels, piloted heart-shaped patches bearing
"Kick Ass," and across the waistband: "PAZMAN."

Pazman was one of us, his skin was dark bronze
And his hair was gelled hard as rock.

Thing with Paz though, was his nose kept changing
Shape[5], something we never saw on Stallone.

Ronnie put a guy to sleep with one shot, Pauly D
Hit another clean in the nose[6]. I bet he did it for you Paz.

I bet he did it for you.

---

[5] *It only takes 9lbs. of pressure to break a nose*. "The Tanned Triangle." Paul "Pauly D" DelVecchio. *Jersey Shore*. MTV. Season 1, Episode 2. 3 Dec. 2009.

[6] *I hit him clean right in the nose, that's the best place to hit someone.* The Tanned Triangle." Paul "Pauly D" DelVecchio. *Jersey Shore*. MTV. Season 1, Episode 2. 3 Dec. 2009.

Tan Tax[7]

Some dressed up
like Indians.
Seagull feathers
stuffed under headbands
because Kenny said
the Pilgrims used
that trick, he remembered
from 7th grade History.
Most just liked the idea
of a party, liked breaking
bottles and throwing them
into the harbor.
Liked floating down
the channel on
looted tanning beds,
pumping their fists
in protest to the beat.
To be stripped
of their color, to whiten
to ghosts: first they come
for our tans,
next our pecs, our abs
of steel
ground to flour.
A bright idea:
The Jersey Tea Party,

---

[7] *The following individuals shall be excluded from the indoor tanning tax within this bill: Snooki, JWoww, The Situation and House minority leader John Boehner.* White House Correspondence Dinner. Barack Obama. C-SPAN. 1 May 2010.

without tea
except for Long Islands—
They went for
the bulbs:
Fluorescents,
Incandescents,
Neons,
Energy-savers…
unscrewed every
single light in town
and added
them to the harbor.
The water turned to glass.
When night came,
they had to learn
to reinvent fire,
that it wasn't just
for cigarettes. In the morning,
hung-over, pale and pasty,
they had to make due
with shoe polish.
They let their shoes dull
to shine light
on their new black faces[8].

---

[8] *Doc Thompson, a fill-in host for Glenn Beck who intoned in March, "I now know the pain of racism.* Aizenman, N.C. "*'Tan Tax discussions include allegations of reverse racism.*'" www.washingtonpost.com. 8 July 2010.

N-Words

I. Take Back Theory

They erase the arcs
Of watermelon,
Unbraid the coarse hairs
Of rope,
Recoil the crack
Of spray from a fire hose
By calling each other
N*****.

II. U.N.I.T.Y.

In the picture, Kelis
Made herself a centaur
But with the legs
And paws of a B****.

III. El Museo del Barrio

When Edwin wanted
His folks to commandeer
S***, his folks said (hell) *No* in
English and en Español.

IV. White the Power

The Revolution cussed me
Out, called me Liberal,

Well-Intentioned,
White Boy, and with that
Fed a juicy cog to The System.
Poor Revolution gone
~~Wrong~~. Poor Well-Intentioned
White Liberal Reclamation League.

V. Mutts

I'm afraid the war
In our DNA has annulled
All potential of slurring us.
I'm afraid the war
Our skin tone has hammered
Into every other color has
Exonerated us from mockery.

VI. Traitors

The Revolution has us wrong.
For each tanning bed
Switch turned on
Another flag burns.
There's nothing more un-American
Than trying to be
Less White.

VII. Guido

My father was lucky.
Not so long ago
He walked to Catholic school
With his boys

And they were called
Waps, Guineas, and
Guidos by the black
Kids they threw rocks at
And called *N*******.

Guido

The boys with the thick necks
Don't know about L'Isola delle Lacrime.

They can't imagine having nothing
To fill a mouth with, a mouth that could tie

A knot with a fig stem. Say "fisherman,"
They think "fishnets."

Say "La migliore parola e quella che non si dice.[9]"
They say, "huh?"

They call themselves Guidos.
They call themselves Italian, even if they are

Irish, Polish, Spanish. The aunts and uncles
Of Italian America are outraged.

But they've forgotten too. Forgot how the simple
Addition of a tomato can change things.

Forgot that in Europe and Italy,
Guido is a badge of honor.

My father was the King of Mt. Pleasant,
And they called him Uncle Guido.

But to Uncle Guido's uncle, that word was
A stick, was a brick. Hard to find the sweet

---

[9] The best word is that which is not spoken.

In a word that made it hard to find work.
Still, the Guidos fill up the television screen

With fighting, with sex, with mouths like Albanians.
They don't even know how to operate an artichoke—

(& I don't know how to pronounce my surname
With a chē. Lost the keys to grandfather's mouth.)

To have a whole culture simplified by
Us, to be reduced to meat-a-balls,

To muscle and pink gel, is unacceptable
To the aunts who made it from Brooklyn to

Patterson, the uncles who crossed the line
From Cranston East into Cranston West.

In this country, a mortgage buys distance.
Their kids study in California, theater, philosophy,

And in the restaurants they own,
Mexicans revive their Nonna's gravy.

They hold a protest, they host colloquiums[10],
They try to disown this remixed manifestation of them.

They flex the (expensive) muscles in their heads,
Postulate, draw circles around the

Shape of hair, the minstrel show they reluctantly
Share a vowel with like a sweat rag.

---

10 Tricarico, Donald. Guido: An Italian American Youth Style. John D. Calandra Italian American Institute. New York City. 21 Jan. 2010.

Guido

We thought you
Were dumb
Until we needed help
With the carburetor.
We made fun
Of the impeccable
Posture
Of your hair
And your MC Hammer pants
Your Z Cavariccis
Your "Bad Boy Club"
Decaled IROC-Z
Maybe because we
Couldn't pull off
All that bravado
Or our parents wouldn't
Let us
And it looked like you had
Big balls
Of tumbleweed
Stuffed under your Big Dogs t-shirts
If tumbleweed
Was hard as muscle.
You were yoked
You were tan and
There were still traces
Of immigrant
All over your quick slant
Your big mouth
Your cheat sheets

Because you were still
2nd generation,
While we were
One grandparent
Closer to first college graduate—
But you were the ones
We wanted
To have our backs in fights and
Because we all
Went to Bishop Hendricken together
You did,
And you were the boys
Who came to Easter
With my silk-haired cousins
So I consider you Family.

Down with the King

I've asked to be down with
You, Eggplant. To be down
With the slight curl
Of your skin when baked,
Like shiny black marble black
Marble glazed with cocoa
Butter. To be down with all
Of You, plural You, like how Tony
Says your name, like he does
Shrimps. Or You fried, You roasted,
You miso-glazed. You high on
Tahini and Baba Ganoush-ed.
When I weaken You, when I suck
Out your muscle in a 108-year-old
Sauce, say *my* Name, call me
Friend. It's because I love You
Parmed, hoagied, Rollatinied that
I treat you this way, my sweet
Comic aubergine. I abhor the
Metaphor that exploits your name
In Sicily. I'll go with ancient
Indian: "King of Vegetables,"
Solanum melongena! Outta space!
Sometimes long and curved like
Ganesh's trunk. Sometimes fat and
Round like Ganesh's belt.
You deep black purple silly-
Named Eggplant. When I bury
An egg in the ground, no chicken
Sprouts, no Eggplant, so how

Did You get that name?
Of course, for the white variety,
"Easter White Eggplant,"
Missionary Caucasian Eggplant,
Always the white that drives
The stake of names for You poor
Bruised Eggplant. Call me the slurs then,
I'm not offended, I'll be that
Eggplant-lover
Eggplant-lover.

Little Waves

My

father

said I'm

gonna live

by the streets

and die

By the streets,

And he did.

My father said I said

By the streets and die by the beach

I'm going to live

I

said

I'm going

to live

By the beach

And die

by the beach,

Till I drown.

Live

I got the best blowout

From sea to shining sea, the seas rehearse his hair eternally. Pauly D

in the country

From sea to shining sea,

said whatever happens

the seas rehearse his hair eternally.

his hair eternally.

hair eternally.

Pauly D said whatever happens happens happens

Pauly D said whatever happens happens happens in the country.

Wind conjures
Waves
Wind conjures
Waves
Wind conjures
Waves

Wind conjures
Waves

Like my dead father would, I sleep with a fan
blowing on my face

dead father would, I sleep with a fan blowing on my face

And wake
With a horseshoe
Crab
On my chest.

horseshoe horseshoe horseshoe horseshoe
crab crab crab crab

I think

If I **fuck up**
I think
Some**thing** bad'**s** gonna happen
If I fuck up
To me,
And that's just the think
Something **bad**'s gonna happen
I need,
To me
Holding my breath
In a submarine.
And that's just the think
I need,
Holding my breath
In a submarine.

I think
If I fuck up
Something bad's gonna happen
To me,
And that's just the think
I need,
Holding my breath th**ink**
In a submarine.

I think
If I fuck up
Something bad's gonna happen
To me,
And that's just the
I need,
Holding my **breath**
In a submarine.

I th**in**k
If I fuck up

Something bad's gonna h**a**p**pen**
To me,
And that's just the think
I need,

H**old**ing my breath
In a submarine.

I think
If I fuck up
Something bad's gonna happen
To me,

And that's just the **thin**k
I need,
Holding my breath
In a submarine.

Can't do nothin' right, like trying to save the lobster by putting it in a bowl of tap water and feeding it worms:

Can't do nothin' right, like trying to save the lobster by putting it in a bowl of tap water and feeding it worms:

Snooki said
That's why I **don't eat**
Frickin' lobster
Because they're alive
When you kill it.
It worms.

Snooki said
That's why I **don't eat**
Frickin' lobster
Because they're alive
When you kill it.
It worms.

Snooki said

That's why I don't eat

Frickin' lobster

Because they're alive

When you kill it.

It worms.

In Ron's juice
Is Stoli,

In God's juice
Is Holy.

In Ron's juice
Is melon,

In God's juice
Is Heaven.

In Ron's juice
Is ice,

In God's juice
Is Life.

In Ron's juice
Is Stoli,

In God's juice
Is Holy.

In Ron's juice
Is melon,

In God's juice
Is Heaven.

In Ron's juice
Is ice,

In God's juice
Is Life.

In Ron's juice
Is Stoli,

In God's juice
Is Holy.

In Ron's juice
Is melon,

In God's juice
Is Heaven.

In Ron's juice
Is ice,

In God's juice
Is Life.

In Ron's juice
Is Stoli,

In God's juice
Is Holy.

In Ron's juice
Is melon,

In God's juice
Is Heaven.

In Ron's juice
Is ice,

In God's juice
Is Life.

Heaven

melon

Stoli

God's juice

ice

Ron's juice

Life

Holy

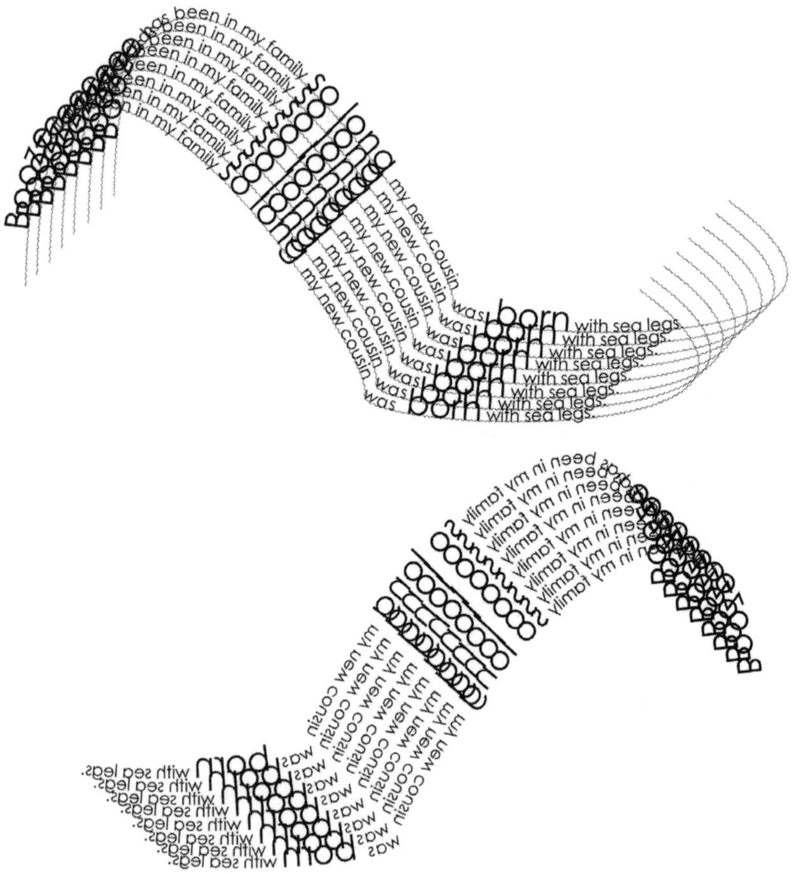
Booze has been in my family
so long
my new cousin was born with sea legs.

The Letter Spelled Ronnie's head In between A dune Of breasts. The one regarding My betrayal Was written in sand, Each grain A tear drop Falling up and Down Through the elbow Of two glass Teardrop. **Spelled** Ronnie's head In between A dune Of breasts. The one regarding My betrayal Was written in sand, Each grain A tear drop Falling up and Down Through the elbow Of two glass Teardrop. **Letter** Spelled Ronnie's head In between A dune Of breasts. The one regarding My betrayal Was written in sand, Each grain A tear drop Falling up and Down Through the elbow Of two glass Teardrop. The Letter Spelled **Ronnie's** head In between A dune Of breasts. The one regarding My betrayal Was written in sand, Each grain A tear drop Falling up and Down Through the elbow Of two glass Teardrop.The Letter Spelled Ronnie's head In between A dune Of breasts. The one regarding My betrayal Was written in sand, Each grain A tear drop Falling up and Down Through the elbow Of two glass Teardrop. The Letter Spelled Ronnie's head In between A dune Of breasts. The one regarding My betrayal Was written in sand, Each grain A tear drop Falling up and Down Through the elbow Of two glass Teardrop.

The Letter Spelled Ronnie's **head In** between A dune Of breasts. The one regarding My betrayal Was written in sand, Each grain A tear drop Falling up and Down Through the elbow Of two glass Teardrop. The Letter Spelled Ronnie's head In between A dune Of breasts. The one regarding My betrayal Was written in sand, Each grain A tear drop Falling up and Down Through the elbow Of two glass Teardrop. The Letter Spelled Ronnie's head In between A dune Of breasts. The one regarding My betrayal Was written in sand, Each grain A tear drop Falling up and Down Through the elbow Of two glass Teardrop. The Letter Spelled Ronnie's head In between A dune Of breasts. The one regarding My betrayal Was written in sand, Each grain A tear drop Falling up and Down Through the elbow Of two glass Teardrop. The Letter Spelled Ronnie's head In **between** A dune Of breasts. The one regarding My betrayal Was written in sand, Each grain A tear drop Falling up and Down Through the elbow Of two glass Teardrop. The Letter Spelled Ronnie's head In between **A** dune Of breasts. The one regarding My betrayal Was written in sand, Each grain A tear drop Falling up and Down Through the elbow Of two glass Teardrop. The Letter Spelled Ronnie's head In between A dune Of breasts. The one regarding My betrayal Was written in sand, Each grain A tear drop Falling up and Down Through the elbow Of two glass Teardrop. The Letter Spelled Ronnie's head In between A dune **Of breasts.** The one regarding My betrayal Was written in sand, Each grain A tear drop Falling up and Down Through the elbow Of two glass Teardrop. The Letter Spelled Ronnie's head In between A dune Of breasts. The one regarding My betrayal Was written in sand, Each grain A tear drop Falling up and Down Through the elbow Of two glass Teardrop. The Letter Spelled Ronnie's head In between A dune Of breasts. The one regarding My betrayal Was written in sand, Each grain A tear drop Falling up and Down Through the elbow Of two glass Teardrop. The Letter Spelled Ronnie's head In between A **dune** Of breasts. The one regarding My betrayal Was written in sand, Each grain A tear drop Falling up and Down Through the elbow Of two glass Teardrop. The Letter Spelled Ronnie's head In between A dune Of breasts.

Good,
right
?

In terms of God,
If I'm wrong I'm
wrong, If I'm right
I'm good, Right?

In terms of God,
If I'm wrong I'm
wrong, If I'm right
I'm good, Right?

Everyone must love
The Situation.
I don't see no
Gringos
Rowing a driftwood
Lifeboat
With a palm frond
From South Beach
To
Cuba.

Wind conjures
Waves. Like my dead father
Would, I sleep
With a fan
Blowing on my face
And wake
With a horseshoe
Crab
On my chest.

My father said
I'm gonna
Live
By the streets and die
By the streets,
And he did.
I said
I'm going to live
By the beach
And die by the beach,
Till I drown.

There was a ring deep
In her skull
Like her skull
Was a champagne glass,
And it
Sounded like
A wedding band
Crashing onto the nights(t)and.

Everyone

I think
If I fuck up
Something bad's gonna
happen
To me,
And that's just the think
I need,
Holding my breath
In a submarine.

Pauly D said
Whatever happens
Happens
I got the best
Blowout
In the country.
From sea
To shining sea,
The seas
Rehearse his hair
Eternally.

must

love

Can't do
Nothin'
Right,
Like trying
To save
The lobster
By putting
It in a bowl
Of tap water
And feeding
It worms.

Snooki said
That's why I don't eat
Frickin' lobster
Because they're alive
When you kill it.
It worms.

The

Angelina said
I'm a bartender,
I do, like, great things.
When a shot
Glass disappeared
Into a pint glass
The hurricane
Left no one
Standing.

Booze
Has been in my family
So long
My new cousin
Was born
With sea legs.

In Ron's juice
Is Stoli,
In God's juice
Is Holy.
In Ron's juice
Is melon,
In God's juice
Is Heaven.
In Ron's juice
Is ice,
In God's juice
Is Life.

The Letter
Spelled Ronnie's head
In between
A dune
Of breasts.
The one regarding
My betrayal
Was written in sand,
Each grain
A tear drop
Falling up and
Down
Through the elbow
Of two glass
Teardrops.

Situation.

T-Shirt

You're 1 of 3 Jewish girls
You're from Cherry Hill and
You push a sea foam
M3 convertible because your daddy
Owns a liquor store
Your aunt has a shore house
She's in Boca so you and
The gals drive over the bones
Singing from New Egypt to
Neptune City singing the same
Four songs for four hours
In the bumper to bumper
Until the beach spreads open
For you like a hot clam
The sun has forgotten about corn
It heats crops of Joy-z girls
Laced with coconut
Ronnie wants to pound out
Every girl in Seaside[11] like girl was milk-fed
Veal but instead of pouring
Malt liquor over the head like in the
"Nuthin' But a 'G' Thang" video

---

[11] Analogies for Sex:
"pound it out" : sex :: mallet : cutlet
"nail it" : sex :: hammer : nail
"screw it" : sex :: Phillips head : screw
"bang it" : sex :: knuckles : door :: index finger : trigger
"smash it" : sex :: masher : potato
"beat it up" : sex :: Pacquiao : opponent
"kill it" : sex :: America : Islam

He pours Marsala wine and deglazes
You who forgot you're older
Than the Geneva Convention
Older than the Lighthouse of Alexandria
Older than the Side Headstand
Older than four lines
Scratched into Hera's ankle
Older than Green Tara with a jewel in her palm
That is an eye
Because you never saw the
Advertisement reminding you
You're 86 trillion years old and
In your corner is every prophet's
Tongue hanging like
Peking duck hanging like Kudzu vines
In an interstellar garden
But you forgot
So tonight you'll get got—
But not before you go
To the T-shirt shop
That can put any words
In any order across the bosom
Of American cotton
To say what you mean and you
Mean to say today: I Love[12] The Situation.

---

[12] Ronnie asked Samantha
If she wanted to smush.
Samantha got the equation
Right, replied, *hold me tight*.

Fuggedaboutit

The drama
on the dance floor
— 108 magnums
of hairspray,
the pumping of fists
like the disco ball
was a speed bag
they were trying
to reach —
was much more
interesting than Mike
"The Situation"
gulping a ghost-faced
Guidette under
an electric palm tree
stage right,
keeping the candle
lit inside the globe
they've made of
their mouths —
and I think about how
we've been inoculated
against intimacy,
made making out cliché
merely the B-side
to getting laid —
till we hardly even notice
the fire in the corner,
the hot coils
of tongue melting

their faces off
until there is nothing
left to remember.

Pauly D Shows Off His Jewels

Family Jewels were once
Metaphor—a red velvet pouch
For our progeny, where our
Future waited to lift a bronze torch
Under our Name, waited to spell it
On the world's marquee
In glittering gemstones.
Today we throw out the poetics.
Today The Forum is in Los Angeles,
Is in Tokyo, is in Bayonne NJ.
Today everything is caricature:
Boobs and lips and tits in cartoon
Operandi. This is the age
Of vagazzling, of reality with
Boom mics and B-roll.
As the apparition held the microphone
Over his bed, Pauly D dug into
His painted jeans and pulled it
Out: a bull's head with a stud
Through the nose.

Guys are douchebags and I hate them all. They don't know how to deal with women. And I feel that's why the lesbian rate is going up in this country.[13]

Lesbians Rising

For every uncle who wants every nephew to bang everything[14]: zoo creatures[15], DTFs[16], Gatorade bottles[17], for every lie white, or purple-black, or Hep-yellow that robs a woman's intuition — the gift Venus lodged into the XY-heart like an Alba madonna, for every douchebag, scumbag, or dirtbag who roll calls you trashbag[18], Staten Island Ferry[19], dirty little hamster[20], for every cheater, deceiver, trickster, fraudulent rat, swindler, every prick-dick-son-of-a-bitch, for every son who has bore *bitch* on his tongue like spit: a lesbian gets her wings.

---

13 "Breaking Up." Nicole "Snooki" Polizzi. *Jersey Shore*. MTV. Season 2, Episode 4. 19 Aug. 2010.

14 *My uncles want me to just come here and bang everything. But I kinda want better-quality girls.* "Going South." Vinny Guadagnino. *Jersey Shore*. MTV. Season 2, Episode 1. 29 July 2010.

15 *I necessarily didn't want to bring back any zoo creatures whatsoever. These broads probably smelled the food at the house.* "Just Another Day at the Shore." Mike "The Situation" Sorrentino. Jersey Shore. MTV. Season 1, Episode 5. 31 Dec. 2009.

16 *Down To F**k*, "The Letter." *Jersey Shore*. MTV. Season 2, Episode 5. 26 Aug. 2010.

17 *Mike would bang a Gatorade bottle if it had a pulse at this point.* "Good Riddance." Ronnie Ortiz-Margo. *Jersey Shore*. MTV. Season 1, Episode 3. 10 Dec. 2009.

18 *She just doesn't want to feel like a trashbag because she has a boyfriend and she kissed me with her tongue.* "The Tanned Triangle." Paul "Pauly D" DelVecchio. *Jersey Shore*. MTV. Season 1, Episode 2. 3 Dec. 2009.

19 *Angelina is just like the Staten Island ferry. It's free and everybody gets a ride* . "Déjà Vu All Over Again." Mike "The Situation" Sorrentino. *Jersey Shore*. MTV. Season 2, Episode 12. 14 Oct. 2010.

20 *You dirty little hamster.* "Dirty Pad." Mike "The Situation" Sorrentino. *Jersey Shore*. MTV. Season 2, Episode 9. 23 Sep. 2010.

You Can Stay and Get Your Ass Beat or You Can Stay and Get Your Ass Beat[21]

It's like a street shaped
Like a dumbbell, dummy.

& the \säb\ is either all pedals
Or all brakes. Get it?

& the trees lining the street
Are walls of ocean, are hanging gardens
Blooming Shark Lilies.

The options are pretty simple:
Lose-Lose.

The options are Boston Red Sox
1918-2004, the clouds over The Monster
Are a nor'easter named The Bambino.

Let's call it an egress-less window-less tree house.
Let's picture it a two-way cul-de-sac:
A back-to-back cul-de-sac. Get it?

That's how I felt, when a double dead end
Landed in my phone,
To bring me the news,

---

21 *You wanna stay, you can get your ass beat. Stay, get your ass beat. Stay, get your ass beat! Stay, get your ass beat! Sleep with one fuckin' eye open! I'm going to make you sweat it out, I'm going to make you sweat it out.* "The Hangover." Jenni "JWoww" Farley. *Jersey Shore*. MTV. Season 2, Episode 2. 5 Aug. 2010.

That lasts ever since
Every sixty seconds
Of every day
For almost two years now.

If this memory was taffy
It'd keep stretching from that minute
To the rest of my life,
The longest ribbon of salt water
Forever ever.

With options like these
Weight falls off like hubcaps.
With options like these
I learned to chameleon glass.

Link together two oxymorons.
Cogent the phrase "beat up the beat."
This is how it feels, regardless
Of the fact's face, pimpled and drowned.

On the show,
After the options were presented,
I yelled at the TV,
C'mon, get yer ass beat.
I talked to the box,
I whispered, *stay*. I know the drill (and
The Novocain)—
Two roads emerged,
I know what's at the end
Of each one.

The Shirt Before the Shirt[22]

I miss the shirt before the shirt,
or the shirt before that even: the shirt
before the shirt before the shirt:
the amuse-bouche shirt.
The shirt before the shirt is steak tartar,
is fried calamari, is Caesar salad, if we use
metaphor. If not, for "The Situation,"
it's pragmatic: functions to catch
spray-tan particulate matter,
sweat, runny hair gel. Like a paper
towel for fried chicken—
I miss the shirt before the shirt
that read "7" on the back: had shadows
under the armpits.
There was the shirt before the shirt
that was lifted-up-and-inside-out
by Amy Hess
in the backseat of a Chrysler LeBaron:
a Catholic school uniform button down,
which had to come off first. A dirty shirt.
Still spotless compared to now's shirt,
with too many wrinkles for its
age, with mythology taped
to its back. The shirt before the shirt
that poured Napa Valley
into parabolas showed no

[22] *I got the fresh kicks, I got some jeans, I got the shirt, but I ain't wearing the shirt when we go out. This is the shirt before the shirt.* "The Hangover." Mike "The Situation" Sorrentino. *Jersey Shore*. MTV. Season 2, Episode 2. 5 Aug. 2010.

mistakes even when spotted
with stains: was folded perfect before
it all changed. I remember the shirt
before the 48th shirt ever, the 47th
shirt, the fist one after the last one
to catch pureed pea spit-up.
The 47th shirt had a whale
on it, a whale shooting a plume of
water from its spout, and on top of the plume
of water was a fisherman
in a rowboat, and all these shirts
later, I know what it feels like
to be that fisherman.

In this type of situation man, you need to separate the two sets of girls, and then you have to separate the hippopotamus from her good looking friend.[23]

Extracting the Hippo

If the boys
haven't evolved
past Kingdom Animalia,

with their horse head
charms bleeding
off a blinged out

food chain,
despite the croc-Visine
behind Ray Ban mirrors,

they know nothing
but to allegorize
you hippopotami.

My language, meant for
breaking, has only given me limp words
for reconciliation.

Has given me the sound
of an Indian dress, but without
golden threaded peacocks.

It is time for quit saying
and start doing.
It is Hammertime.

Lost Love,
when you see me approaching
with a diamond wrench,

23 "The Letter." Mike "The Situation" Sorrentino. *Jersey Shore*. MTV. Season 2, Episode 5. 26 Aug. 2010.

Don't run.
I've come to extract
the done wrong.

I started by learning to diffuse snakes,
milking fangs into grapefruit,
sucking out the venom.

I worked with rabbits (therapists),
went to meetings (anonymous),
hid doves (god) up my sleeve.

I practiced stacking
up mansions of cards
and Jenga-ing the Jokers.

When I manage to jimmy out
your pain, I will place it
in a glass box.

It paces the square like
a white tiger. It glows in there
radioactive.

I cover the box
with a red silk drape.
Spin it 3 times.

Instead of hocus pocus,
I keep it culturally relevant,
say *badda bing, badda boom*

before lifting the silk.

Escapism

When word got
To him
It was much too late
To stop the flood,
Or board up
The windows of
(Wolf)
Mouths —
Some called for
Damage Control —
But he could only
Think of self-
Preservation,
Or self immolation,
Or stare down
The long barrel
Of a bottle
Of Lorazepam
Because the sentences
Sounded like too
Much
Treble
Sounded Click
Sounded Babblefish
And the story
Wore snakeskin
Wore a blame finger
With a mani,
So instead of dying
He planted

His ass in the ripped
Polyester of a plaid
Couch
And thanked
God for a world
He could fit into
A square,
For plasma
Congealing to reality,
For Ronnie
Pounding the bass
Or a face,
Giving him
A fist
To live in.

5 Grenades[24] (Homage & Apology)

I. Lorde

Two Coke bottle
bottoms dispel
the blindness. X-ray
technician sees the
insides. The ghost
writer hides an omen
in the syntax. She was factory
worker, librarian, Tougaloo
bulldog, feminist.
Feminist isn't the right
word though. Two girls kiss
in East Harlem. Lorde takes
the name Gamba Adisa—
Warrior: She Who Makes Her Meaning Known.

II. Indira

They didn't want
to believe you were
anything
more than a Dumb Doll.
Gungi Gudiya.
Tagore named you Priyadarshini,
"pleasing to look at,"
but we all know
that poets are dogs.
So easy for a Nixon to call

---

[24] *Ron is at the club hooking up with grenades, which is a bigger ugly chick, and land mines, which is a thinner ugly chick, and ... loving life.* "The Hangover." Mike "The Situation" Sorrentino. *Jersey Shore*. MTV. Season 2, Episode 2. 5 Aug. 2010.

you an old witch. So hard
for you to finally crack
beneath 30 rounds
of bullets.

III. Minaj

Nicki, how many
goats did you slide
a sacred blade
beneath the neck of,
how did the blood
fall from a rooster
and what rum was spit,
what was burnt
and offered
or poured
into ornate cups
and set before golden
statues for you
to get all that power?

IV. Coretta

It must have been
a fire blanket in you.
It must have been
a hydrant full of holy water,
musta been momma
calling down from heaven.
To see how far you'd come,
little ol' you, didn't want
to make a fuss.
When he was away,
you'd let the soprano out.
When he took off his ring,

before climbing on top of
not you, his ears rang all night.

V. Nana

You built up a tolerance
to standing all day, to taking
orders and pouring coffee
and bussing dishes and
sweeping floors and giving
money again for the last time
to a son who drains it
into his arm, to surviving
the heat from a kitchen's
engine or papa's
mouth, and you still give
regardless
of if we call you
by your name, Rose.

VI. Epilogue

The TV, the radio,
or the fossils etched
into our groins
can not apologize
for calling you grenades,
landmines, pigs, sluts, hos & bitches
after eating your mother's lentils.
After two-timing, and three-timing, and
four and more. After you trace columns
down our backs with your fingertips
while we watch SportsCenter
and the only other words
we have for you is:
Don't Stop.

About the Author

Michael Cirelli is from Cranston, RI. He is the author of *Vacations on the Black Star Line* (Hanging Loose, 2010) and *Lobster with Ol' Dirty Bastard* (Hanging Loose, 2008), which was a *NY Times* bestseller from an independent press and was featured in the "Debut Poets" issue of *Poets & Writers Magazine*. His work has appeared in *The Best American Poetry*, *Hanging Loose*, *New York Quarterly*, *Texas Review*, *Poetry Daily*, *World Literature Today* and *King Magazine*. He is the Executive Director of the award-winning youth literary arts organization, Urban Word NYC, and has authored two poetry curricula, *Poetry Jam* (Recorded Books, 2010) and *Hip-Hop Poetry & the Classics* (Milk Mug, 2004). He has also appeared on HBO's *Def Poetry Jam* and *Brave New Voices*. He lives in Brooklyn, with his 9' *Peter Pan Slug* surfboard.

Penmanship Publishing Group was created by writer and performance poet, Mahogany L. Browne. As a freelance music and entertainment journalist, Mahogany found the hierarchy of the literary world painfully silent and unyielding. She created Penmanship as the answer to the performance poet's publishing problem. Penmanship's purpose is to become the anchor for publishing performance poets and live artists in the hard to crack literary world.